The Journey of a Soul Sister

Part 1

The Birth of a caterpillar

By Inge'Marie Harris

Copyright © 2022 Inge'Marie Harris

ISBN: 9798459596311

DEDICATION

I DEDICATE THIS BOOK TO MYSELF, FIRST AND FOREMOST, TO HAVE THE STRENGTH TO SHARE MY JOURNEY NEXT,
I dedicate this book to the world because my story is not just for me; it is for everyone!

CONTENTS

ACKNOWLEDGMENTS

I would like to thank everyone I came in contact with in my life, no matter what stage I was in. I have learned something from each one and every one of you!
Thank you, the person reading this, and thanks for wanting to go on this journey with me!
Lastly, but most importantly, I want to thank my Ancestors and God for helping me on this Journey!

Introduction

Do you know our souls existed before you were a thought? You know they say you will go through some shit before getting to where you need to. You will have a story to tell or some bull shit like that. Hey, do I have a story to tell AND A JOURNEY to share? Guess what? I know I haven't yet reached where I am supposed to go.

This Journey has been no joke, and I am still on it to keep it real with you. But on the way, I was fortunate to find happiness with myself and my soul and never give up!

Also, don't compromise what I stand for! No fuck nigga, no weak bitch, and most importation, My Money!!!
Sit back, get your tissues, drink, and blunt, bible, sage, crystals, or whatever you need to get through this book
Forever the Journey of a Soul Sister!

1 609 MAINE STREET.

*How can you not feel loved before you even know what
love is?
The noun for Love is
an intense feeling of deep affection.
Verb
feels deep affection for (someone).
So why was I not giving those feeling like a child and
young adult, but I was always willing to give it?*

609 main street is an address I will
never forget! My mother and father
were married for ten years. My mother
had one daughter before she married
my dad. Jay and I are seven years
apart, and then my parents had
another daughter together. My sister
Bria is two years younger than me.
Lastly, she had one more girl, but not

From my dad; my baby sister Nick is five years younger. Yes, my mother and father were still together! My father was a drug addict and alcoholic who was fighting so many demons!!

His mother was a murderer right in front of him when he was five years old, and when the police came, they found him holding his mother's brain matter in his hands, crying, saying mommy wake up. Also, he was never good enough in my grandfather's eyes. Their relationship was very abusive. Not a lot of love was shown to him as a kid. After trying to beat us half to death, he always told my sisters, mother, and me that this was all he knew. My father worked a lot of dead-end jobs, including construction housework. My mother worked as an engineer for various hotels in the downtown Baltimore area. Some mornings depending on if there was a

Fight or not with my parents; my mom would wake us up before school to get us dressed. My father would be downstairs drinking his mad dog 2020, cutting up his white powder, and then snorting it up his nose this was his morning routine so he could function. *(Later in life, I learned white powder was cocaine, and I would be selling and cooking it in years to come)*

The first time I was involved in a drug transaction, when I was six years old, was when my father took me down the street to his dealer's house to get his drugs. He would tell me he needed this to be happy to hide the pain he was going through. *(When I got older, I would understand.)*

Then we would go home, and he would put his drugs in the Bible in the house. *(Years later, my mother would find where he kept it.)*

As my siblings and I were heading

out the door to get on the yellow school bus *(in the county, we had yellow school buses that would pick us up on each corner in the neighborhood)*, my father would say don't fuck up! He would call my mother and say kiss me and don't die today if you know what's good for you. She would kiss him and tell, Him she loved him.

I would always wonder why and how you could love someone who tells you not to die, but in the same breath, I loved my father.

For the first nine, maybe ten years of my life, the neighborhood I grew up in was hell. We lived in a Segregate area, and I went to a primarily all-white school where I never fit in or at home.

There were only three black kids in my class, including me. I was the only light-skinned long-haired girl in a class named Inge'Marie. The teachers made fun of me. I remember my second-grade teacher called me Inge bing buga, and then the whole class would call me that for years to come. My third-grade teacher MS. Mickey, yes, MS Mickey told me just because I was light skin don't think I would get a pass in this school. She was a tall, dark-skinned lady that was so mean to me, and I never knew why. I only had two friends in elementary school. Their names were Kelly and Ashlee. *(Name change)* They were twin sisters. We were outside playing on the monkey bars; Kelly said, 'our mother said we could only be friends with you, Inge, because you are a pretty nigger." I knew the word Nigger was terrible, so I pushed Kelly off the monkey bars.

Let's get back to where I lived and the people entrusted to keep me safe and didn't. For as long as I can remember, I have been emotionally, mentally, and sexually abused for years! A lot of it was in elementary school.

I remember the first time my father hit my mother in front of us. I had to be 7 or 8 years old, and he drilled her for coming home too late from work *(little did I know in years to come I would get hit for that exact reason by someone I believe loved me.)*, and she did nothing. My face had the look of so much disgust. How could you allow someone to hit you and you don't hit them back, but in the same breath, tell me if someone hits me, and hit them back!

She wouldn't even move!! He told her to jump, and she would say how high! I felt like she was so weak.

Why wouldn't she fight back?

So that would become an everyday thing, her getting beaten on like it was normal. I remember stopping to care and just knowing this is what love is; it got to the point that everyone in the neighborhood knew but turned a blind eye. We, as black people, have this thing that if it has nothing to do with us, we keep our mouths shut! Not knowing that we could probably save a life if we just helped.

We always went to the babysitter's house before and after school and in the summertime. This lady watched everybody's kids in the turn station. Maybe she watched some kids in the day village, primarily those living in the turn-station.

For the respect of this lady, I will not use her real name; I will say Ms. Lady; Ms. Lady would always pinch me for any and everything. She would say things to me like you; luckily, I am fucking your father.

I can't believe he married your mother over me. Keep in mind she already knew what was going on in my home. She would force us to watch her soap operas, like Guiding Light and

Days of our Lives.

I honestly think that's why I hate those soap operas and had difficulty letting my kids go to daycare. She had three kids living in her home, and they always were mean to all of kids. I would have a snack, and they would take them and call me names like half-bred.

Do you remember when schools would have fundraisers, and you had to sell pizza or cookies? I did a fundraiser and sold over 100 dollars in pizza and cookies one year. I was so excited just knowing I would get a prize. I had never won anything at that time in my life. The day we had to turn in the money, the school closed, so I spend the day at Ms. Lady's house.

I was so upset because school was

close, and I wanted to turn in the money so I could win. Ms. Lady knew I had the money and wanted snacks. She told her oldest child to take me to the bus and get snacks. Her oldest child came to me and said, "I know what will make you happy" I said really? She said," Yes, let's go to the yellow bus and get snacks with the money you have, and they will give it to the school.

I thought what she said was true, and trusting her, we did just that. (*The Yellow bus was an old broken down school bus with all kinds of snacks and candy like a coroner store*) When my father came and picked my siblings and me up, I heard him talking to Ms. Lady, asking about the money I was supposed to have for the fundraiser. She told him that I had spent the money at the yellow bus.

Inge' Inge Inge 'Marie, come here now!

You don't hear me fucking calling you!! I was so scared I ran out the back door down the field to hide, but I turned around, and my dad was right behind me!

He placed his hands on the back of my neck, dragged me into the house, and said to my mother, "you need to beat her, or I will beat your ass." "She spent the money for school when she could have just given it to me so I could get high," He said.

I am not mad; she gave me a beating. I spent money that I shouldn't have spent. I was upset for two reasons. Neither of them asked me what or why I did what I did. (Of course, she beat me, in case you were wondering.)

After the beating, I was sent to bed without dinner. I lay in my bed mad at the world, thinking, why am I alive? I just wanted to die. I begged God to kill me and take me away from this pain.

The next day I went to school. I kept writing on my classwork at my desk; I wanted to die. Later that day, I was asked to come to the offices, and there were two white ladies from child protective services asking me why I wrote I want to die on my paper. I looked and told them because I wanted to. I hate my life. Keep in mind I was in elementary school.

(So now that I am older and I hear a story of a kid killing themselves, I understand why and it brings me back to the time I try to kill myself)

They asked me why and I began to tell my story and what was happing in my household. To watch my father do drugs, beat my mother and siblings, and be molested.

Later that day, CPS came to my house to do an interview. My mother told my sisters and me that if we didn't want our father to kill her, we would say nothing was wrong, and Inge (me) made everything up because I got in trouble about the money.

The CPS workers pulled us one by one into a room and asked questions. When it got to me, I said I made it up.

I was just upset because I couldn't get my way.

Cps left my house, and my father beat my ass and told me if I ever went back and ran my mouth again, he would kill my mother and me. Whatever goes on in this house stays in this house. He said.

I knew right then and there asking for help was pointless. If I wanted out, I had to find my own way!!!

2 CRYING OUT FOR HELP

Per CDC Centers for Disease Control and Prevention,
Suicide is death caused by injuring oneself with the intent
to die. A suicide attempt is when someone harms
themselves with any intent to end their life, but they do
not die as a result of their actions.

The beating would continue every day. I became so used to it, just getting ready for what will happen next.

At this point I knew asking for help at the time was useless, and no one would save or help me escape the pain and hell. I felt the next best thing was just to end this life.

"This can't be life? Why me? What did I do to deserve this? Why don't my parents love me? Why does my father hurt us, and my mother does nothing?

He would get so upset with us for doing what kids do when sitting for too long.

One day, he got so frustrated because we wouldn't sit still and watch the Ten Commandments that he handcuffed us to a handrail and beat us. I peed on myself and kept saying, "In my head," I hate him. "I want to die." "I hope he kills me."

Unfortunately, he did not kill me. *(Thank god he didn't)* Later that night, I was thinking about how I could die? Sunday night I had made up my mind, and I knew I would do it. I knew I was going to kill myself.

The following day, as we all got ready to go to school, my father did a line of cocaine, wiped his nose, grabbed his mad dog 2020 strawberry banana drink, and loaded us all into the car. As my father and mother were on the way to drop us off at the babysitter's house, I opened the car door on the road and jumped out!

I wanted a car to hit me and kill me. My parents pulled over and rushed me to the hospital. They were asking me why I would do that. I didn't respond to them. I kept looking in a daze because I couldn't believe I was still alive.

Why didn't I die? The doctors came in, made my parents leave the room, and asked me why I jumped out of the car? I said I don't know; I knew if I told the doctor why he wouldn't help, just like everyone else that knew what was happening to us. So I lied and said, "I didn't know why." The doctors asked me repeatedly; I still said the same thing.

Later that night, I went home and was told to go to my room.

As I was in my bed, I talked to god. I asked him why you saved me? Why leave me in this hell? Why why? I don't want to be here! God never answered me at the time,

(But later on in life, he showed me why he didn't take me away from here.) (So I say to anyone that suicide can start at a young age, and I understand why some people end their life.)

The following day we got up, and everything repeated as if it was a typical day. Weeks went into, months went on, and nothing changed.

It was summertime, and I remember we used to have cookouts and my mother's family would come over, and we would play bones *(domino)* and spades. It was always a good time.

I used to have a favorite aunt who always came to the cookouts. She was the baby of my mother's sister's Aunt

Jay. She always told me I was beautiful and that one day I would push through the hell I was living in at the time.

Aunt Jay asked me why I jumped out of the van, and I told her the truth.

She cried and made me promise I would never do it again. I promised her that but little did I know I would break that promise not once but twice more years later in life.

3 CRYING NEVER SOLVES ANYTHING

. Have you ever noticed that crying is weak? What are you crying for? How about this one, fuck you crying for shut that shit up. Keep crying, or will I give you something to cry about? The whole time you already give me reasons to cry!

I hate this saying, but I love it all simultaneously. My father didn't have sons at the time, so I guess it was his way of making us tough and prepared for this fuck up world we live in.

I remember him punching us right in the chest and saying, "you bet not cry because, in this world, you are going to receive pouches like this almost every day in your life." He would also say crying is for the weak. I am not raising any weak-ass bitches. Crying will not fix anything. It's pointless even to be able to cry. Why cry?

Stand on whatever happens to you, or say, because only you can control what happens next!!! In some weird little way, it made sense to me. I would carry that attitude for years to come; to be honest shit, I still act like that. I don't believe I ever really had a healthy cry.

They say you need a healthy cry that's good for the soul. Still, whenever I feel like I have to cry or my eyes get wet *(yes, when my eyes get wet?)*
I am ready to fight. I feel like somebody needs to feel this pain because who the fuck are you to even make me feel this way? I am not weak;

I am the strong one.
Back to my father and his methods to make you strong, he used to call it!

My sister Bria, nick, and I had just gotten out of the tub one late afternoon. My father would always sit in the bathroom and smoke his newport100 while we were in the tub. I was in charge of ensuring my sister got out of the tub and dressed.

My sister Bria went back into the bathroom and said she had to poop, so I didn't think anything of it.

Five minutes pass, she returns to the room, and we get dressed and ready for bed. My father comes and busts in the room with a loud bang as we are lying down.

"Which one of you little bitches smokes my cigarettes?" We jump up, looking in a daze, scared. I know I didn't do it; my sisters couldn't have done it; he repeated, "Which one of you little bitches smokes my cigarette?"

We continued to just stare in fear as he yelled. Next, he walked over, grabbed us, and asked us to blow in his face.
He was checking to see whose breath smelled like smoke. He did my baby Sister Nick first; she was clean; next, it was me, and I was clean, but when he got to Bria, she blew, and there it was, she did it.

It put our father into a rage like no other. He grabbed Bria by her hair and dragged her into the bathroom. I ran out of my room after her, where she smoked his cigarette because I knew he would hurt her.
He said, "Inge watch this, and you are next because you should have watched

her." I stood there in fear and did what I was told.

My father turned on his clips, put the clippers on Bria's head, and stated, "Bitch, you want to smoke like a man. Now I am going to shave your head like a man."

Out of nowhere, my mother came into the bathroom to stop him. He slapped her across her face, and my sister Bria ran into our room and hid under our bed. Our father told my mother, "You want to save her, so now you will take this ass whipping."

He began to beat her, and she did nothing and didn't fight back; she just took it. I watched the whole thing and didn't move as he said.

When he was done, he said, "Inge, this is all your fault; if you had just watched your sister, none of this would have happened," as he was lighting his cigarette. He said, "I will be back soon, and told my mother to give him a kiss and clean yourself up."

When he walked away, I ran over to my mother and tried to help her, but she pushed me and said, "It's all your fault; get out of my face; you are just like him." I was so confused; how was this my fault?

The next day came, and we were back to our routine.

My father hated that my oldest sister was not his child and that my mother had another baby before him. He always give her a hard time. We were in the kitchen; he came, drunk and high after dinner. He began to say disrespectful things to my older sister, and she said something back to him and punched her in the mouth.

My sister had braces in her mouth with no wire. When he punched her in the mouth, her braces got caught inside her mouth.

Then he stated, "Run your fucking mouth now bitch."

He called for our mother and said, "Get your smart-ass daughter." Then he looked at me and said, Inge, "why you didn't help your sister when I punched her in the mouth?" I looked, and I started to shake and cry. I said, "I don't know." He said you want to cry? What did I tell you about crying?

"Is this what you will do when somebody does something to your sister or sisters?" You fight; you don't cry or stand there like no little bitch."

Then he punched me in the chest, kicked me up my ass, and told me to go to bed.

From that day on, I knew I had to protect my sister's no matter what, even if that mean I would get hurt.

Maybe a month later, about five girls came to our house to fight my sister Jay. My father pushed Jay and I outside and said fight!

He stood there at the door as we fought the girls. Keep in mind my sister is seven years older than me. The last two times, I cried like a child; once, when I was on a playground with some kids at the turn-station, they ripped my shirt off my back, pulled my hair, and said, "You think you are cute? I ran home crying and my sister Jay said no, stop that crying; it's time to fight.

We went back to the playground, and I had to fight. The next time I cried, I was in the house with my father and sisters, and we were planning to run away. My father came into the room and saw me packing my sisters and my stuff, and he asked, "What are we doing?"

I said, "They are not doing anything; I am doing it." He said, "Okay, smart ass, what are you doing?" I said, "I am packing; we cannot stay here anymore with you!" He said, "So you think you will just pack up the shit I paid for and leave out my door, you ungrateful little bitch?"

I didn't say anything; I kept looking at him in his eyes with no fear, and for a minute, we just looked at each other, and no words were said.

He graded me the next thing I knew he said, "If you want to go, you can go, but you will not take my daughters or anything I paid for out of my house." I said, "I don't care; you can have this stuff, but I'll take my sisters." He said, "Oh, you think you got it like that?" as he laughed. He said, "Let me show you how you are not big and bad and don't have it like that."

He dragged me from our room down the stairs to the front door past my mother. He said, " So Inge, you want to leave, right?" and I said yes. He said okay, take your clothes off. I said, "Take my clothes off?" He said, "Yes, take your fucking clothes off before I take them off of you."

My mother yelled, "What is going on, Inge? Go back upstairs with your sisters. "My father said," Don't you fucking move; if you move, I'll kill your mother right in front of you."

He turned to her and said, "Shut the fuck up and stay out of what I do with my daughter." She shut up and walked away. My father told me, "Inge, take your clothes off!" I took off my shirt; he said, " Okay, take off your pants now," so I did. Next, he said, "Take off your underwear," and I did.

I was standing at the front door naked. He said, "Now you want to go so go." I said, "I couldn't, I don't have any clothes aid, ``so what? Get out!" He pushed me out the door. It was raining so hard outside.

The crazy thing is the sun was still up. I stood there for hours crying cold and naked, wishing someone would save me or god would just let me die, but nothing happened. I watched the sunset, the sky turned dark, and the rain slowed down. Hours later, he let me back in and said, "I bet you don't feel big and bad anymore." "I bet you don't want to leave now?"

"You were out there crying, and what happened? "Nothing! Did it fix your problem?" No! "If you think you want to leave, that's what your life will be like; now take a bath and go to bed without dinner!"

He was right in some sick way, and the lesson stuck with me throughout my life.

    In   a   good   and   bad   way.

4 APRIL 2 1997

April 2, 1997, have you had a date or a day you can remember like yesterday? Well, that's what April 2, 1997, is to me!

At 5 pm, my mother, my two younger sisters, and I drop our older sister off at work. She worked at McDonald's after school and on the weekend. Money was tight, so she had no choice. It was about 7:30 pm, no later than 8 pm; my mother had just given my younger sisters and me a bath and done our hair.

She told us good night. I was asleep and heard the door slam and my father yelling. "You are trying to leave me and take my kids away from me bitch!" "I will kill you first before I let you do that."

Next, I hear him running up the stairs

repeating himself.

I jumped out of bed and thought that this was the day we all would die. I told my sister Bria and Nick to hide under the bed. Until I come back, I am going to help mommy.

I ran out of my room into my parent's room and saw my father having her in a headlock with blood out of her mouth.
My mother looked at me and said, "Inge, call the police." Now she never asked or called the cops on my dad ever in life, so I knew this was real.
I ran downstairs and picked the phone up, and the line was busy.

The phone upstairs in my parent's room had to be off the hook. I ran outside, banging on the neighbor's door with no answer. I ran from door to door; I yelled, "Please help; he is killing her!" A new person was moving in across the street. I ran over and asked her to please help and call the cops. My father was killing my mother, and she said to come inside.

I went inside; the lady handed me the phone, and I called the cops. I tried to leave and return home to help my mother, but the lady was not trying to let me out of her house.

The next thing I saw out the window was my mother and father coming out of the house, fighting. That was the first time I had ever seen her fight back. She picked up the shovel and hit him with it over and over. At that moment, I was so happy to see her fight back. Somehow he got the shovel and hit her in the face with it.

My mother fell to the ground, and he began to beat her. It felt like he was beating her for hours. The cops finally came, and my father ran and hid in a shed at the back of the house, and the cops came and got him. The ambulance came and took my mother, and she went to the hospital.

The doctors told her she would have died if she had taken ten more minutes of that beating. She had broken ribs, face swelling, and one eye closed shut. When she came home from the hospital the next day, I could barely recognize her. My sister and I slept in her bed for about a week. My father got bailed out of jail the next day.

My father kept coming pass the house for weeks, watching our every move. Until one day my mother came home and said we had to move! We packed up all we could fit into our blue Van, and we left Baltimore.

From that day on, I knew I would fight if a man ever hit me. Or try to kill him.

5 THE MOVE

The next couple of years didn't get any better. We moved to North Carolina, stayed in a hotel for three months, and got put out because my sister had mental issues.

We lived in a shelter for one day. We had to leave because this man tried to steal our stuff. At this point, that was the first time I had ever been homeless. We slept in the Van for three weeks; when my mother had to work, she would drop my sibling and me off at a park with food. She would tell us don't tell anyone our business, and I would be here to pick yall up after work.

If it rains, we have to sit at the park under one of the Gazebos. I remember washing up at rest stops to stay clean. (*If you've ever been homeless, and I mean homeless, sleeping outside or in a car, not sure where your next meal is coming from, it does something mentally to a person*).

After a month of doing that, my mother said, "we were moving back to Baltimore." We moved in with my mother's first cousin Ted, his wife CeeCee, and their two children. I can't remember how long we stayed with them.

Next, I remember we moved to Baltimore city, 2710 West Franklin Street. We lived there for like three months. I remember being scared to go to a new elementary school with city kids. I walked into a new school on my first day of 5th grade. I looked around and saw black kids, teachers, and staff.

I have never seen that before. I was

signed up for a pal center and participated in many activities. I felt like we finally got a home. (*Little did I know we would be moving again?*)

One day, I left the recreation center after having a good old time. I was on my way home, and a friend stopped me, and they said, "Your house is on fire." I ran as fast as possible; my mother and two younger siblings were standing outside with the fire department.

We lost everything, and now we are homeless for the second time. I felt like we were right back where we started when we would ever catch a break. I found a school, my voice, and friends who liked me.

We stayed in a motel and then moved to southwest Baltimore, 223 South Furrow St. In that area, it was called the section. It was mostly a white area when we moved there. I wasn't scared at all because mostly all my life, I was around nothing but white people; however, I didn't know they were racist. Within a month of living there, we had a massive fight with the white people on the block.

A week after moving to the section, I was enrolled in Samuel Fb Morse Elementary; we called it #98; it was a mixer of black and white kids. The white kids were nice to me, but the black kids were mean.

They used to bully me. They would say why do you talk and dress like a white girl. Push me, take my snacks. They also would ask why I hang with white people. It was easy because the black girls didn't like me.
Duh,

Keep in mind I have never seen an issue with how I dress or talk. I thought they were weird because they spoke broken English and would have their hair cornrowed and with fake hair in their heads. But still, I was not mean at all.

My mother had signed me up for an after-school program called kids grow. The lady MS Cookie was a god-sent. She knew I was different, took me under her wing, and helped me fit in and stand up for myself.

One day at lunch, a girl named Bug was always bullying me, but I had enough this day, and I hit her in the face, and we began to fight. I didn't lose the fight either. The funny thing is that a year later, we became excellent and close friends in middle school.

That same day my two younger sisters broke into the house and didn't go to the babysitter's after school and were taken to foster care, and my mother would spend the next three years fighting the system to get them back.

My oldest sister was living her life, and I would try to follow her around and do what she did, but she was not having it. I used to get so mad when her boyfriend and her friends came over because she would switch up and be mean to me.

So I said, hey, I will be the little sister from hell. I would fight her friends and cuss her boyfriend out. I would steal from them, eat their food, you name it, and I did it. Cause she should have put me first. She knew our mother was only worried about her man and my other sisters. At this point, I felt alone, lost, sad, and pissed. I had made up my mind that I was out for blood.

I will do what I want when I want, and nothing and no one was going to tell me different. I would run the street, cut class, start school fights, drink liquor, and smoke weed by age 12. At home, I wasn't given the love and support I needed; we had already been thru Hell, so why not?

The next thing I knew, my oldest sister was put out of the house because she was 18, and my mother's boyfriend at the time told her she had better put her out!

Once again, I never understood why or how you could let a man tell you your child has to leave, and you listen. My sister would stay up the street at a friend's house for a little and then move in with our Aunt Yee.

I remember visiting my sister at my aunt Yee's house, and she our cousin Dee Dee were in a room talking, and all I wanted to do was come into the room with them. Our cousin Dee Dee always hated that I was Jay's sister. She always felt that I took her place with my sister, but that was not true for me, and my sister was and still is not as close as they were. So she would be mean to me and say I was found in a dumpster. That's why I was different from them, and my mother hated me. I was just like my dad, and I will be just like him when I get older.

So at this point, she had no idea how nasty I had become; she tried that mean shit that day. So I waited and listened outside the door to their conversion and told her mother all the nasty things she did to boys. I also called her a dirty ass slut, and she was going to die because she had sex. I laughed the entire time she got in trouble. It felt so good to see her cry.

The next thing I knew, my oldest sister told me she was going into the military. My response was, "so you're going to leave me alone?" She promised me when she got her stuff together, she would come back and get my younger sisters and me, But she never came back to get us; she started her own life with a new family and friends.

All while I was stuck in hell. I know now that I am older how that can happen, but I could not understand at the time.

I believe that's why our relationship is the way it is now, me being in my 30s and Jay in her 40s and not being as close as some sisters are.

I told myself if I ever had daughters, I would make sure they were best friends! *(Guess what, I had daughters, and they are best friends.)* A short time after

Jay's move and being the only child left in the home, little did I know my whole life would get even more out of control.

6 NEW FAMILY,

YES, I SAID NEW FAMILY
NEW FAMILY IS WHEN MEETING PEOPLE WHO ARE
NOT **BLOOD-RELATED**, AND THEY BECOME
FAMILY, OR YOU HAVE A BABY **WITH** SOMEONE
AND BOOM, YOUR FAMILY RATHER YOU LIKE IT OR
NOT.

Now at this time, I was still the only child in the home, and my mother was still chasing after a man and still fighting the courts to get my two little sisters back from foster care.

So it just left me to take care of myself. Every day I continued to do what I wanted if; it was hanging out to three in the morning, hanging up Hollins street with my home girls, down the section on the block chilling with the niggas, or with La'shay, and Ready

Drinking, smoking weed, fighting, you name it we were doing it. The only thing I wasn't doing was having sex, but that wasn't too far off.

I remember my first day up Hollins, my new family aunt Meak that was the same age as me, asked me to come to her house. So I did, and it was so many people outside.

She introduces me to everyone. It used to be like 13 of us out having fun, drinking, smoking, and maybe fighting each other, depending on the day. We were around the ages of 12-15 years old. Yes, 12-15 years old, and if you are wondering, I was 12 years old.

One day I went up Hollins street like any other day, and there he was., this beautiful brown skin, short cut, boy with a pretty smile, and bowlegged.

He was standing on the corner with the other D-boys. (*A D-boy is a drug dealer)* but this one caught my eye. I asked my aunt Meak and my home-girl Bug who is that? They both said at the same time, "who bitch?" I said, "Him right there bitch!" They both said, "O girl, that's DeShawn" at the same time. "I said DeShawn is so cute." My home-girl bug said, "I am about to call him over here," and "I said no, don't do that bitch." But it was too late; she was yelling across the street, "Deshawn come here, yo!

He said "okay, here I come Bug." I felt like I had to shit, and my heart was beating out of my chest! He walked over and said "what's up bug?" Bug said "shit, my home girl Reds *(that's me, a nickname Hp gives me).* Think you are cute." DeShawn looked at me, smiled, and said, "You think I am cute, huh?" I said, "Yeah, you're alright."
He smiled more and said, "Walk with

me." So I walked with him, and we talked. I found out he had a baby that was about to be one. Found out that he was six years older than me. He had a car; it was a station wagon.

After that day, He would pick me up, take me to buy food, and call me his little girlfriend. You couldn't tell me anything. I was on cloud 9.

One night I didn't come outside, and everyone was hanging out at my aunt Meak's house, drinking and smoking. DeShawn was there. I got a phone call saying bitch get up here Deshawn is in the room with Meak.

I left out the back door of my home and ran up Hollins street as fast as I could. I got there a little late, and they were already done. Just know I flip out on both of them.

As far as Deshawn and me, we fell off. (*But years later, I spent the block on him to see what it was hit for, and maybe we could pick up where we left off. Giving were adults.*

Well, I am here to tell you the dick was good but to be honest, that's all I wanted; now that I am older, we are into different places mentally. Have you ever just wanted to have sex with someone to say you hit it? Or you realize you don't like this person and physical wear off?)

Well, that was me with him and some other man. (*We will get to that in a later chapter or part 2 of Journey of a soul sister.*)

After that whole thing with Deshawn, I started hanging more down the section at my house, 2223 south Furrow St, Monroe Wilhelm man, all around southwest Baltimore. I guess you can say I was a street runner. I even hung out in Brooklyn pig town, the village, Douglas's projects, and the avenue (*Pennsylvania Avenue*).

Now that I think about it, it's not hood I didn't go. Let me tell you; my house was the house to hang out in; my mom worked all the time, chased after a man, and fighting the foster care system to get my little sisters back. So it was like I was rising myself and the streets helped. It was lonely at times. I wanted to have love and those family things you see on Tv or what some of my friends had, but it didn't work out that way for me.

As time went on, I was always outside and barely in school. I used to have a boyfriend named Ant, and I thought we would be together forever, but then he broke up with me out of nowhere one day.

I was hurt. I told my home-girls and homeboys like I didn't know what happened. A friend that Ant and I had in common was Zeek. I would do nothing but talk to him every day

about Ant until Zeek told me to get over it. He doesn't want you, and I should give him a try. It took me by surprise. I didn't even think Zeek liked me. Ant doesn't want me, and Zeek does. I know I can make Ant mad so fuck it let's do it.
From that day on I was Zeek's girlfriend. (*Little did I know Zeek would become the father of my firstborn son.*)

Every day I was at Zeek's house or outside on the block with the d-boys. Zeek's house was so much fun; we could drink alcohol and party, and it was like everyone that lived in Zeek's house all had girlfriends, and they lived there as well. Zeek's mother was like his home-girl; she would let us do what we wanted. We smoked with her, drank with her, and partied with her, you name it that was the place to be at 14.

One day I wasn't feeling well, and I told my home-girl Rendy how I was feeling; she asked me whether I got my period. I stated I don't know; I don't think so. So we went to the dollar store and bought a pregnancy test. I went home and peed on the stick, and two lines popped up saying I was pregnant.

Don't let anyone tell you they don't work because it works. I was scared I didn't know what to do. I told Zeek, and he was like what do you want to do?

Keep in mind he was only 15 years old. I said I don't know. He said well, whatever you want to do, we will do.
A week went by, and I got a call from my older sister Jay that she was coming to visit with her new baby boy and her husband. She wanted us to meet them. I was excited to meet

them, and most importantly, I wanted to see my sister, explain what was going on, and ask her what I should do.

Well, my sister, her baby, and her new husband came to visit, and it didn't go the way I thought it was going to go. Here in Baltimore, we love seafood and crabs. (*Omg, Monroe st. had the best crabs back then.*) We went to get some and sat at my mother's dining room table, my sister Jay, her husband, our mother, her boyfriend, and me. As we were eating the crabs, I started to feel like I was about to vomit! I got up and ran to the bathroom, and yes, I vomited.

When I got back to the table, my mother said, "You bet not be pregnant." "I said no, I am not even having sex." (*Now yall know that was a lie; I just told you last week I took a test.*)

My mother said okay, "I will make you a doctor's appointment, and we will see." The following week I had an appointment, and they confirmed what I had already known that I was pregnant. To top it off yall I was 13 weeks. I had no clue I was that far along. Only 14 years old couldn't even take care of myself; now I will have to take care of a baby.

When my mother found out how far I was, she told me to get out. She wasn't raising any more kids that weren't hers; my younger sisters were coming home, and I needed to go. She also said, "This would not be a good look for your sisters or a good example; you're just like your father, a disappointment.

I replied okay, I packed my stuff and left and moved in with Zeek and his family. We told his mother the same day, and she asked Zeek was this his baby. Zeek said yes, that's my baby. Yall, I was pissed; why would she ask him if it was his baby or not! But now that I am a mother of two boys, I understand why she asked.

When my god-brother found out that I was pregnant, he asked me how I would take care of myself and the baby. He said you are not old enough to get a job, and I know you will not depend on a nigga to help you. I asked him what I should do then. He said, "I would give you some weed, and you can sell that." Then I said what my cut is?

First, he said 80/20. I said hell no nigga. I've been around yall long enough to know that's bull shit. He laughed and said, "OK, I will do 60/40; remember, you work for me now, and if you get caught, you didn't get it from me."

At that point, he started teaching me the game do's and don'ts. I hated bagging up; that] was the worst part.

I asked my god-brother," why do we use these bags?' He said, "What do you want, jugs?" I said, yeah. He said, "That's going to have come out of your cut." I said, "hell no!" As I was working for him and learning the game, I was going to school every day not because I had to but because that's where I made the most money. The money was coming so fast, just off weed. It was so addictive. Whenever I do something, I try to be the best at it or make a name for myself.

After six months of working for my god-brother, I saved up enough money to get my own weed and not work for anyone. My god-brother was so happy for me that he introduced me to his connection. It was all up from there. As my pregnancy was coming to an end Zeek and I started fighting more and more. You know when you are young you think that you and your baby daddy will be together forever?

Wishful thinking; we were kids!
I would put my hands on him every time he said something dumb or he was in a girl's face.
One of the biggest fights we had was when I was eight months pregnant, and he was outside on Wilkens Ave in a girl's face, which happened to be his other girlfriend. Mind you; I was still living with him and his family. How dare he play with me like that?
However, we got into a big fight, and I called my mother and asked if I could move back into her house. She told me if I moved back, I would have to pay rent. I said I don't care; I will pay whatever.

That same night I moved back into my mother's home at 223 south Furrow St. Her heat didn't work, and she had to heat her home with the stove.

Have yall ever done that before? Now that I think about it, we could have died from Carbon Dioxide poisoning or a house fire. What was I to do? I didn't have anywhere else to go.

Months later, on January 13, 2003, I became a mother at 15 years old to a Baby boy. He was 7lbs5.6oz 19incs long. The most beautiful person I have ever seen in my life.

I got the feeling when I held him in my arms I never knew before the love that came so fast I never felt before. On that day, I promised him he would be better than me. I tried to give him anything and everything I never had. I will love him so much that he will never have to question if he was loved or not.

His father and I tried to make it work for almost a year after we had our son, but, to be honest, it didn't work. I had to grow up fast, and he didn't.

He was only 16, and the streets and girls called his name. To tell you the truth, the money, the niggas, and the streets were calling me.

Zeek had a cousin name Black; Black had a girlfriend named Tae. Tae and I grew close; we were with each other every day. She introduced me to her cousins and home-girls, who were way older than me at the time. I still was the baby of the group.

Tae, her cousin, and home-girls showed me how to get money from these niggas. Every Sunday up druid hill park, the 12 clock boys *(here in Baltimore are known as the niggas that ride dirt bikes)* and niggas with the cars would be outside. It was the place to show off and get you a nigga or a bitch.

Man, the amount of money I saw these niggas give to the girls, and they didn't have to fuck, I was like, sign me up. I got a baby to feed and sisters to raise. We used to drink gin knotty head man that shit would put hair on your chest lol.

I got so many stories that would be a whole other book, but I have to thank them because they were some real hustlers. As we all know, when you play that type of game, people change, and issues start to happen. All of us hanging out came to an end. For the same reason that motivated us to get money and these niggas.

My home-girl, Tae, and I were still

hanging together. One day Tae was hanging out with niggas she had just met, and I was supposed to go that night, but I didn't have a babysitter, and thank god I didn't have one.

That night Tae ended up getting locked up and doing time for being at the wrong place at the wrong time. She held her own and didn't snitch. I never forgot her and was always there when she needed letters, pictures, phone calls, and money on the books; that was my bitch! *(Come to think of it, anyone I knew who got locked up could always call me.)*

Tae called me from the women's jail one day. I was like, I don't have any niggas, and Tae was like, I'm going to hook you up with someone. I was like, who, and she said my cousin, Mark. She had me call Mark on three-way and said, "I want you to meet my home-girl" "He was like, what she looks like?" Tae said, "She's your type; just come see her." He came that same night to see me. He was with his older brother and another homeboy.

He was fine, yall brown skin and long dreadlocks; he looked like Lil Wayne *(y'all know how Lil Wayne looked when he came out with the song go DJ. Yes, lord in my Kevin Gates voice, lol!)* His smile and laugh would light up a whole room. After our first day of the meeting, he was at my house almost every day for like seven months, maybe? We both were still running the streets, so that was short-lived. We would hook up from time to time until 2018. In the meantime, I am running the streets and taking care of my one-year-old son and my two little sisters. I was hanging with my bitches from Hollins. We would be on Monroe and Willham, and Payson Street every day. That's when I met Dre from my home-girl, Bug. Bug, at the time, was messing with his cousin. The cousin asked Bug to hook Dre up with someone.

Bug called me on three-way with Dre. Dre had just come home from jail, and he was on the box. He couldn't come outside unless he was going to school, but he wasn't. That day we stayed on the phone for like eight hours, and then he said you should come over to my house tomorrow. I said sure, where do you live and he said Payson Street.

I was like, hell yeah I can do that. I'll be there around 7:30 pm. I arrived at Dre's house around 8:00 pm and had no idea what Dre looked like. He opened the door, and he was light brown skin shorter than me. Dre was not all my type, but our conversion was incredible, and I am doing a favor for my home-girl Bug.

So as the night went on, he started telling me his life story and why he was on the box. I started thinking, I liked him. He has been through some hard times, just like me. We both just want love and a family. We are both hot heads and know how to get this money. I went home before the sun came up, and for the next five months, we were with each other every day, and he was my boyfriend!

After the 5th month of us going together, I called his cell phone, and he wasn't answering. I called Bug. I said Bug; you talk to Dre; she said I didn't. I said bitch go with me to his house. I am about to pop up on him. (*Now, I always get a feeling when someone lied or was being sneaky; back then, I didn't know what to call it, but I was always right and still right to this day.*)

Bug and I met at Dre's house and were knocking at the door with no answer, but we could hear people in there. Bug like "yo, wait by the alley for the back door and see if someone comes out the back." As I was waiting and she was bagging, Dre opened the door and say "what yall doing?" as I was making my way to the front, I saw a girl coming out of his backyard.

So I started to chase the girl, and he ran outside trying to stop me from chasing the girl. Dre and I got to fighting, and it was over between him and me. When you are young and immature, you want to get back at the person who hurt you.

My home-girls and I would come on Payson Street even more and hang with them niggas on the block. Just to make Dre even madder. While doing that on this day,

April 27, 2005, was when I met a demon disguised as my savior. My first love, kryptonite, and narcissist King Marcus   himself!

7 TRAUMATIC BONDING

Trauma bonds are emotional bonds with an individual that arise from a recurring, cyclical pattern of abuse perpetrated by intermittent reinforcement through rewards and punishments. The process of forming trauma bonds is referred to as trauma bonding or traumatic bonding. Trauma bonds have severe detrimental effects on the victim not only while the relationship persists, but beyond that as well. Some long-term impacts of trauma bonding include but are not limited to remaining in abusive relationships, having adverse mental health outcomes like low self-esteem, negative self-image, and increased likelihood of depression and bipolar disorder, and perpetuating a trans-generational cycle of abuse.[4][5][8][9] Victims who traumatically bond with their victimizers are often unable to leave these relationships or are only able to do so with significant duress and difficulty. Even among those who do manage to leave, many go back to the abusive relationship due to the pervasiveness of the learned trauma bond.[10][11]Wikipedia

The day I met King Marcus, he was getting out of a car. He had a burgundy hoodie, white tee shirt, blue jeans, and air max Nike. King

Marcus was light brown skin, golds in his mouth, 6ft tall, 280 pounds, and he was a "D-boy" When I saw him, I said to my home girl Tee, who is that? She said girl, that's King Marcus, he crazy girl; don't say anything to him.

(Whenever I hear the line, ooh girl, that nigga crazy, don't say anything to him from a young Jezzy song, it brings me right back to the day I met King Marcus).

I wish I had listened to her; we are all a little crazy, right? I couldn't help myself. I had to talk to him. I went over to my homeboy Mont and said put me on with him; he is so cute.

Mont said you sure that's what you want? I said yes, that's what I want". He said "okay I got you" (*I should have asked him why he asked me that.*) Later that night, King Marcus hit me on the Nextel *(if you ever had a boost mobile phone back in the early 2000's you know what that means?)* Come right thru my line. King Marcus said what's up? I said, who is coming right thru my line." He said, "Girl, you know who this is." I began to laugh because he was right. I knew exactly who it was. "I said yeah, I know who this is."

King Marcus said, "What are you doing? I said shit on the block and was about to go home in a little bit. "Why," what's up?" He said "on the block? Your little ass is funny. "My nigga Mont and I are trying to come thru." "Are your home-girls still with you?" I responded," Yeah, we are all going back to my house, and how am I funny?" King Marcus said "because you are now, get off the block and go home because I am ready to come see you now." Yall know what I did? I went my ass right home. I turned right to my home-girls and said, "Bitches we got to go.

King Marcus and his homeboys are coming to my house." My home girls were like bitch tell them to bring some weed and drinks. I called King Marcus back and said, "yo get some drink and weed." He said, "Alright."
King Marcus, his homeboys, Mont, and Chess were at my house within thirty minutes. That night was so much fun.

King Marcus and I smoked, got drunk, and talked the whole night. I found out we both had mommy issues.
His mother and mine put a man before their kids. We both never had our father in our lives the way we would have liked. We both were hustlers and knew how to get money.

We both were homeless before, and both were the Black sheep of our families; we both only wanted a family and to be loved. We both knew that night we were what each other was looking for, and we would give each other what we needed.

The next day King Marcus moved in with us. He didn't even ask; he just told me he was living with me here. I let him. It wasn't a second thought; he wanted to be a family. I wanted a family, and he and my son were it. My heart and mind were saying all the hell you went through is over.

You have someone who will never hurt you and wants the same things you always wanted, so Inge 'Marie, Don't fuck this up! Let's keep in mind I still had niggas I needed to cut off. I was still outside hustling, raising my little sisters and son.

For about a month into the relationship with King Marcus living together, he let me run the streets and move as I was always moving. I was still entertaining another man while I was outside because they still were giving up the money I didn't have to fuck, and to be honest, I loved the attention. It was hard letting go of some old habits. I wanted my relationship with King Marcus.

Now, remember I told yall my home girl Tee said he was crazy, and I just thought it was a joke. Well, I am here to tell you it wasn't a lie.

One day I was sleeping, and King Marcus kissed me and said I would be back. I didn't think anything of it. About an hour later, he came back into the house and woke me up.

He said "Inge Inge Inge... You don't hear me fucking calling you?" *(The tone and the way he said my name, I knew I did something wrong, and he brought me right back to the day my father found out I spent that money.)*
I got up and went downstairs, and I

was skating and so scared my heart was beating out of my chest. One thing for sure, two things for sure, I stood my ground.

Me: yo why the fuck are you calling my name like that? I was fucking sleeping

King: Yeah, who are you talking to? While you were fake sleep, I went through your phone and was texting the nigga you've been texting off the AVE.

Me: why the fuck would do some bitch ass shit like that.

King: because you belong to me, don't ever forget it. !

Then he handed me a bag and said, open it. I opened it and inside it was five cellphones, money and drugs in the bag.

Me: where did you get this from?

King: From that bitch ass nigga you was texting and the niggas he was with. I pulled on him like I was you coming to see him, and I pulled my gun out, and I told them to kick that shit out, you know what time it is

King: now, let's see how you going to talk to him moving forward.

All I could do was look in shock, lost for words.
King said, don't look stupid now. He pulled out his gun, pointed it at me, and said, " Talk to other nigga, and I promise you, you will be the reason that nigga will never breathe again.

Then he kissed me and said "I love you, and let's go to bed." I did just that.
That night I knew he was not to be

played with. I never want anyone to get hurt behind me.

The next day he said "you know what?" No woman of mine will be hustling and running the streets. My response was you know I need to make money his response was I got you, I got us.

Only did I know King Marcus' "I got you and us" would turn into 11 and half years of isolation from family and friends, break ups to make ups,
Him disappearing for days and coming back with money and gifts as if he never left. Manipulation, He had a baby with another woman on me; check this out the baby was born in the same month and year as our son.

Me getting my ass beat and fighting for my life, low self-esteem three kids later, Jail, homeless, extremely jealousy,

Lack of empathy for others Breaking the law, and trying to take his life and my own!

8 IN LOVE WITH A NARCISSIST

Narcissistic personality disorder — one of several types of personality disorders — is a mental condition in which people have an inflated sense of their own importance, a deep need for excessive attention and admiration, troubled relationships, and a lack of empathy for others. But behind this mask of extreme confidence lies a fragile self-esteem that's vulnerable to the slightest criticism.- Wikipedia

Marcus: "I love you, you don't need anyone but me, and you hear me, Inge?"

Marcus: "I said I got you. I told you wouldn't want for anything, Inge? Inge you love me, right?"

Me: "Yes, I love you, Marcus."

Marcus: "Then prove it."

Me: How I thought I was. You don't believe I love you, Marcus?

Marcus: I believe you love me but not how I love you.

Me: What do I have to do to show you I love you?

Marcus: You are not going to do it.

Me: Marcus, what do I have to do?

Marcus: Okay, give me a baby! I want a son.
(Keep in mind I was only 17 years old and already had a 2-year-old son.)

Me: Are you for real?

Marcus: Yes, I told you, you don't love me like I love you.

Me: Marcus, we are not married yet, and we still live with my mother and sisters.

Marcus: Inge, don't I pay bills here? Put money in your mother's pocket and yours? Don't I watch your son so you can go to school? Don't I help take care of your sisters as well?

Me: Yes, Marcus, but,
Marcus: but nothing Inge you will be 18 soon, and when you do, I promise I will marry you on your birthday.

 I will move all of us out of the hood I got you. See, I knew you didn't love me how I love you, Inge.

Me: Marcus, okay, we can have a baby. We started that same day. For the next three months, King Marcus was a god sent, I thought. He was bringing that money into the house my family and I did not want for anything. We could have whatever we wanted. With him bringing in the capital, King Marcus would disappear for days at a time and wouldn't answer the phone. Of course I didn't know any better. I thought that's what you had to do to bring that money in. He would come back and have bags and bags of cash, gifts for the whole house.

(Later in life, I learned what he did to get that money. So will you in part 2)

King Marcus kept his promise to my family and me and we wanted for nothing; he also gave my mother money to put up so we could move and she could buy a home; he also had me open a bank account for cash just in case he would say. Also, he had a lawyer on standby just in case he would say.

One day King Marcus and I were sitting at the dining room table, and he said you are a little street smart, but I need to teach you the game. Teach you that a person could never outfox a fox. I said the game, and a person could never outfox a fox; what do you mean by that.

He put a bag on the table with cocaine, baking soda, a measuring cup, a pan, and vales with a red top. Then he said all we need is water. I look like, wait for what, why are you showing me this? He said now you want to act like you don't know what you're about to be doing. I am not going to be doing anything like that.

You said that life was behind me. Inge,

you want more money, right we will be having another baby, so you need to know what to do just in case something ever happens to me and you need to take over. Just then, it was a knock on the door. It was his homeboy C. King Marcus and his homeboy C were real close; you could say two peas in a pod.

When King Marcus would leave for days, he would leave C at our house to watch over us. Marcus says yo C; she thinks I am fucking playing with her. I was like, what the fuck are you talking about? I am not playing with you.

He said "who the fuck are you talking to?" "Inge do you know who I am?" he said I said "what I am talking to you." He said "bitch do you know I will fuck you up?" I said "bitch, who you are calling a bitch." He had his hands around my throat. The next thing I knew, I kicked him in his balls. He let me go, and I said "don't you fucking think I am that type of bitch." Keep in mind that I grew up watching my mother get her ass beat and fight niggas, so hitting him back was an automated response.

Marcus starts to laugh, and I say what's so funny? "You want to fight, right? His response was "I love you." "Yo, C, she is crazy, just like me." Then he said come here and give me kiss me, you know we will fight at times, but that's what happens in a relationship."

"I will never really hurt you, Inge. Inge, you are my life and soul, family, and everything; I am nothing without you," he said. Then he pulls out money and says call your home-girls and go shopping. In my mind, this isn't right, but that's all I ever saw my whole life.

Later that day, when I was out shopping with my home-girls, I told them what happened, and not one of them thought it was an issue. That was the first of many physical altercations between us.

King Marcus knew my weaknesses and how to exploit them. He used my insecurities against me, convinced me to give up things important to me, to make me more dependent on him.

When all this was happing to me, I thought what he was doing was love, right? They tell you to be open with your partner and share your hopes and dreams. They said your partner is to know everything about you so yall can grow together.

My favorite one is to let the man be a man. He will lead you in the proper direction. Oh, how about this one? If he pays the bills, just shut up and take it! Be Lucky; you have a man.

As a result of this in my love life and friendships, I now tell you that I find it very hard to open up and let people in. Also, I don't trust a soul to lead me.

This page is for you to take a breath and get mentally and emotionally ready for the next chapter!

9 If you love me, you will stay!
DOMESTIC VIOLENCE

PHYSICAL ABUSE. PHYSICAL BEHAVIOR THAT IT IS VIOLENT MAY BE CONSIDERED PHYSICAL ABUSE.
EMOTIONAL ABUSE. EMOTIONAL ABUSE IS USUALLY VERBAL.
ECONOMIC ABUSE. ECONOMIC ABUSE MAY OCCUR WHEN A PARTNER TAKES CONTROL OVER THE OTHER PARTNER'S FINANCES. PSYCHOLOGICAL ABUSE.

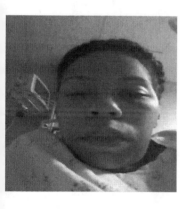

PICTURE OF ME ONE OF ONE OF OUR FIGHTS

Let me start by saying it's never okay to be abused or abuse others.

Abuse is not love. I repeat, it is not love!! Just because you saw it your whole life doesn't make it right! If they hit you once, they will, and I mean they will do it again.

Most times, it starts with verbal. Also, it comes in all forms of manipulation, which is mistaken for love. Leave!!! Never stay; you think it will get better, but it won't! It's only suitable for a moment! Only if someone would have just told me it was not okay!

Your abuser will have you thinking that you are the problem and you did something wrong. Speak up; you will not be embarrassed!!! Your life matters!

Now at this point, King Marcus and I had been together for about four months, and we just had found out I was pregnant. He still would disappear for days and come home like it was cool and say he was taking care of things. He was so happy that I was pregnant. You would think we would be in a better place, but we weren't.

King Marcus and I would call each other out our names so many times out of the day because we both did not know how to express our feelings correctly. I would say, I was the one who was more verbally abusive to him, and he was more physically to me.

You know what, I am not going to lie, I will say depending on the day, it would be him, or it would be me. We both were so cruel to each other when our feelings were hurt. For him, it was always when I didn't do what he wanted me to do. Or if he didn't know where I was. For me, it was every time he would yell or stay out, I would lose it, or when he would say a thing that was stupid to me, I would make him feel less of a man. Who do you think you are playing with? It was always a reaction. It didn't make it right.

However, I always told myself I would not be anybody's bitch! You are not going to talk or do anything to me without a fight. So I would step to this man every time. Knowing the outcome could be death.

Just think about it I watched my mother get her ass beat and talk to like shit and never fought back. Not me, I love you, but I will give you just what you give me. It was like the littlest things would set him off. Sounds, lights, me not listing to him when he was ready to speak, not feeding his ego.

At the same time, he would be the most loving, giving, and sweets man you have ever met. He made me feel like I was on cloud nine and, at the same time, made me feel like I had to walk on eggshells or fight for my life.

The little things would set him off, from a guy looking at me or a hello from a stranger. One day, I was cooking eggs for my oldest son and me. My oldest son Eman was in the living room watching Dora. King Marcus was just walking into the house after being out all night, saying he was on a mission.
Whatever that means.

King: Where's my food, Inge?

Me: What?

King, so you don't hear me? EMAN,

go upstairs and watch tv in your mom mom room. *(Mom is a nickname for my mother)*
My son did just what he asked.

King: Now, Inge, where the fuck is my food.
Me: Your food is where you were at all night. I was putting the eggs on a plate and about to set the table. When King Marcus walked over to me in the kitchen and knocked the food right out of my hand. He grabbed me by my neck and dragged me into the bathroom next to the kitchen.

The next thing I remember is my son EMAN running down the steps calling me mommy, is the food done. King Marcus let me go, and I ran to my son and said no, it's not done. I gave him fruit snacks and told him to go back upstairs while I made his food.

I believe if my son never came back downstairs, he would have killed me.

When I turned around, King Marcus was in the kitchen cleaning up the eggs; he knocked out my hand and said "I am so sorry, Inge, I don't know what happened." "I love you." 'You know I love you, right?' "Inge, please talk to me, please." "I said get out. I can't do this; you have to go."

He said "you really want me to go?" "I thought you loved me; you are pregnant with our baby; we are a family; you are going to leave me like my mother and father did." "We are soul mates, Inge. If you love me, you will stay!"

"I am sorry I never met to hurt you." "I blank out." He said. "You know I got shot in my head, and sometimes this happens." "If you hadn't talked to me the way you spoke to me, I would have never hit you." Don't you love me? I will make it alright.

How much money do you want? You going to leave me just like everyone else? Keep in mind I told yall I would never be like my mother; I would never live her life. I would never stay with a man who puts his hands on me. I always questioned what made her stay.

So ladies, don't ever say never or be so quick and say it won't be you, because you will never know!

So what do you think I did?

Introduction,

The Journey of a Soul Sister
Part 2
The Butterfly Cocoon

Alarm, goes off; its 6:30 am. I roll over and look.

This Bitch didn't come in last night? He knows we got a doctor's appointment this morning. Now I am calling his phone, the phone going right to voicemail.

This nigga is so disrespectful. I told him the next time he stays out; it's over. I get up and go downstairs; maybe he sleep on the sofa. What I was saying to myself. Get downstairs, and his homeboy C sleep on my fucking couch.

Me: C, get the fuck up! You in my fucking house sleep, and this nigga didn't even come in last night?

C: Yo, sis, he didn't come in last night? Clam

down.

Me: Clam down, shit, you know where he at, you know what, that's it! It's over! C, Get the fuck out of my house!! When you see that bitch tell him he lost his family he wanted so fucking much!

C: Sis, wait, something is wrong; he told me he was coming in last night. I think something terrible happened to him

Me: Nothing happened to your homeboy; you are just trying to cover for that bitch!

C: No, he would have told me if it was something else, call the hospital for real, sis. You know what type of shit we are doing.

Me: What? I don't know what type of shit yall be into, but okay, I will call the hospitals.

I call all hospitals in Baltimore

Me: C he not in no fucking hospitals; what type of fucking games are you playing?

C: sis call the jail.

Me: okay,

Jail: Hello, Baltimore City Detention Center.

Me: yes, I am calling to see if my husband is locked up.

Jail: Name

Me: King Marcus

Jail: date of birth

Me: 02/10/19–

Jail: Yes, He's here.

Me: Okay, does he have a bail

Jail: he hasn't seen the commissioner yet.

Me: Okay, thank you.

I hang up the phone. What this can't be life!

ABOUT THE AUTHOR

Inge'Marie Harris was born and raised in the dynamic city of Baltimore, Maryland As a child, Inge exhibited a strong determination and a sense of purpose, which translated into her personal and professional life. Through her grit and perseverance over life's challenges, Inge consistently tries to better herself, and her children, and inspire others she comes in contact with.

Inge aligns with her dedication and passion for community outreach, development, and networking. Inge'Maire has volunteered and participated in Baltimore Autism Speaks Walk. Additionally, Inge'Marie is a huge advocate for young women and teen girls trying to find their way Inge'Marie served as the Service Chair of the National Association of Health Services Executives (NAHSE), Baltimore Chapter. Inge'Marie serves as a board member for the St. Francis Neighborhood Center nonprofit, 501(c)(3), and as a community liaison for Helping Hearts Initiative Non-Profit Organization

Inge'Marie is the author of 3 part series autobiography called The Journey Of A Soul Sister. Inge'Marie is the Ceo & Host of Anythangoes Podcast, Ceo and founder of Journey of a soul sister, Life coaching, Host of Tale of 2 Scorpio IG live Show, and a Host on Chillin with joose Podcast,

Made in the USA
Middletown, DE
27 June 2022

67722212R00064